EVELYN SCHLAG (born 1952) grew up in Waidhofen an der Ybbs in Lower Austria. She studied German and English at the University of Vienna before becoming a teacher in Vienna and, later, in her home town of Waidhofen. She has published a wide range of poetry, prose and short stories since 1981 as well as translations (notably of Douglas Dunn) and essays. An English-language *Selected Poems*, translated by Karen Leeder, was published by Carcanet in 2004, and an English translation of her novel *Die Kränkung* (*Quotations of a Body*), translated by Willy Riemer, appeared in 1998. Schlag's works have been greeted with much critical acclaim, and she has received many awards, including the 1988 Bremer Förderpreis, the 1997 Anton Wildgans Prize, and the Otto Stoessl Prize in 1998. She was Lecturer for Poetry at the Institut für Sprachkunst (2010/2011) and a Member of the Judging Panel for Dublin's IMPAC Prize 2012. In 2012 she was selected to represent Austria in the Poetry Parnassus (held at the Southbank Centre, London). She is a member of the Graz Literary Academy. She was awarded the Austrian Art Prize for Literature in 2015.

KAREN LEEDER (born 1962) is a writer, translator and academic. Since 1993 she has taught German at New College, Oxford and is Professor of Modern German Literature there. She is also a translator of German poetry into English, most recently Volker Braun, *Rubble Flora: Selected Poems* (with David Constantine, 2014), Michael Krüger, *Last Day of the Year: Selected Poems* (2014) and Ulrike Almut Sandig, *Thick of It* (2018). Her translation of Evelyn Schlag's *Selected Poems* (2004) won the Schlegel Tieck Prize in 2005 and she won the Stephen Spender Prize in 2013 for her tra\~ 'ation of Durs Grünbein.

EVELYN SCHLAG

ALL UNDER ONE ROOF

POEMS

translated by Karen Leeder

CARCANET

First published in Great Britain in 2018
by
Carcanet Press Limited
Alliance House, 30 Cross Street
Manchester M2 7AQ

Book design: Luke Allan.
A CIP catalogue record for this book is available from
the British Library, ISBN 9781784102241.

The publisher acknowledges financial assistance
from Arts Council England.

Supported using public funding by
ARTS COUNCIL
ENGLAND

Contents

ALL UNDER ONE ROOF

Translator's Preface

It was always clear after the success of her *Selected Poems*, published by Carcanet in 2004, that Evelyn Schlag and I would work together again. That volume introduced Schlag's poetry to English readers; charted her evolution as a poet across the course of four collections between 1989 and 1992; and won the Schlegel Tieck prize for Translation in 2005. This volume picks up where the *Selected Poems* left off and contains poems from two subsequent collections: her *Sprache von einem anderen Holz* (*Language of a different Stripe*) of 2008 and her *verlangsamte raserei* (*racing in slo-mo*) of 2014. Much has changed in the decade between that *Selected Poems*, which first brought her into English, and her most recent German collection. She has firmly established herself as one of leading contemporary Austrian writers and was awarded the Austrian Kunstpreis for Literature in 2016, among the highest honours that any Austrian writer can receive. She has written four novels; and in 2012 she was selected to represent Austria at the Poetry Parnassus held in London at the Southbank Centre.

Yet her voice, for all the differences that the last decade has brought with it, is still in some senses recognisably the same. It is quiet, elegiac and largely inward, though it accommodates passion, grief and rage. It is mysterious and humorous. It would be fair to say that hers is a singular voice in the Austrian context, without imitators or any kind of school. For all the discretion that also plays a large part in the poems and the emotional vulnerability, there is also a kind of stringency and radicalness that sets her apart: 'find out what you do best / and leave it behind' ('Ars Poetica'). And while it has affinities with the Anglo-American tradition in many ways (notably in its interest in the concrete and in its irony), it is also a voice that runs oblique to the traditions of English-language poetry in other ways, rendering it strange and constantly surprising. At the same time, the two collections sampled here themselves see a distinct evolution in the form of Schlag's language. Earlier work used a variety of recognised traditional forms. These collections progressively loosen the ties of convention, following instead 'long years of that tiny private picking' ('Vita Poetica') and pursuing a more singular inward path. The 2014 collection, *verlangsamte raserei*, for example, consists of cycles of strictly rhythmic poems without rhymes that rely heavily on line breaks and work with often surreal neologisms and playful sound patterns. What is more, they consistently reject the traditional upper-case of German grammatical usage and do away with almost all punctuation. All these things give a new lightness of touch, intensity and freedom to the language. The abolition of grammatical hierarchies also brings an increased ambiguity as lines can be read as connecting forwards or backwards at the same time.

The themes that she returns to are love, memory, landscape and art. Love is the central animating force of Schlag's poetic (and novelistic) world. It appears in all sorts of familiar guises from the charge of the random erotic encounter – 'once I would have said very forbidden things' ('Passenger') – to the intimacy and ordinariness of everyday loving:

> Then you embrace me
> hardly leaving room for rosemary
> or bag. Your face reveals a sudden flash
>
> of how oblique the day is: slanted like a flight
> of steps into the sideheart of the city.

Some of the most touching poems included here are those about marital love in old age.

But, in the spirit of her 2016 novel *Architektur einer Liebe* (An Architecture of Love), the poems do not simply thematise love but also try to echo the shapes we make as we inhabit these various relationships, as 'we search for a new contour' ('Hesitant Prospect').

As in previous collections, childhood memories loom large: sometimes, as in the sequence 'Plaits', also as a way of exploring larger historical events, when the fairy-tale tones of childhood meet with the cartographies of war. Memory of illness too finds its place as in previous collections, but explored with characteristic restraint: 'No Pathos Please'. Many poems present themselves as travel diaries that range through Europe, UK, USA, Syria and Russia, knowingly testing the boundaries of autobiography and fiction. There is also a sequence responding directly to works of visual art, 'The Jewels of Brazil'. But beyond these there is also a powerful sense of the poet negotiating a place within an international artistic tradition. The poem 'If Bohemia Lies by the Sea' is an explicit response to the Austrian poet Ingeborg Bachmann, for example, to whose tortured legacy (most akin in English to that of Sylvia Plath) Schlag responds in a characteristically blunt mode: 'Ok, Ingeborg: that's enough'. Schlag has written elsewhere about her difficulty coming to terms with Bachmann, though it would be true to say that many of her poems do in fact constitute an on-going exploration of this formative influence. Alongside Bachmann readers will recognise encounters with other, especially female, writers: the Austrian religious poet Christine Lavant (1915–1973) provides an inspiration for the bitter anger of 'Conditio Divina', for example. But Anna Achmatova and Elizabeth Bishop are also interlocutors, alongside painters and musicians across the centuries: from Johann Joachim Quantz, eighteenth-century German flautist, to modern American painter Thomas Moran.

If the natural world is a constant in Schlag's work, it is by no means an idyllic refuge. It is marked everywhere by a profound sense of unease and ecological threat that finds sudden catastrophic expression in the wholesale slaughter of the BSE crisis in the UK, for example, or a tsunami on the Atlantic rim. New, though, is the acute awareness of a contemporary world of smart phones, shopping malls and inner-city violence. The changes in the new Europe over the last decade also leave their mark: 'these are moments of political joy / you must lay down in your coronary arteries'. But for all the new logos in the East, the shiny consumer palaces and the dreams of the 'shopperplankton' ('All under One Roof'), Schlag focuses above all on the victims: the widows of the Chechnyan war, the murdered Russian journalist Anna Politkovskaya or the young women forced into prostitution and violence. She offers these images of contemporary life without any explicit judgement, however; rather, her acute understated images do the work. Memorable in this context is the 'littlest girl' at the end of the poem 'Unarmed Civilian Security Service' who watches impassively as the teenage town 'hyenas' engage in a brutal mugging before skipping off, satchel bobbing.

Anyone coming to Schlag's work for the first time will be struck by the power of her images. The poems are conceived as intensely visual concentrates, with often surprising perspectives or humorous angles. For all their attention to the domestic or even frankly banal, this means they are also frequently mysterious. This mystery is enhanced by an often surreal take on language. In both collections, the playful half tones, neologisms and surprising word combinations act as an antidote to the language of media and everyday reality. But especially in the most recent poems, language has taken a further step: becoming less directly referential and following a logic of feeling or sound, rather than of grammar. Poems play through repertoires of overheard voices, with snatches of sense swimming into and out of focus; or pursue associative paths through sound: 'Dowland like download' ('Renaissance Song'); 'cirrus // or circus clouds' ('Cirrus').

As with the previous English volume, I found some of the poems forming in English in my mind even as I read the German; others felt much more resistant to their new home. But overall I have the sense that translating these poems has been more challenging than in 2004, despite the fact that I know Evelyn Schlag's work so much better than I did then, and that the process of translation accompanied many of these poems as they were being written and rewritten over the course of many years. Through all this I have been privileged to work closely with Evelyn herself, who has been enormously patient and generous with her time. We have I think both learned a good deal about this most delicate fetching across between people, contexts, languages and cultures.

Two things are perhaps worth saying. The first is that in finding English versions of these poems I have been particularly struck on numerous occasions by how differently the sense of a line's rhythm works in German and in English. Even if people working in different traditions can agree on the technical scansion of a line (and Schlag has an excellent knowledge of English-language poetry and herself translates), this work has opened my eyes to the different weights and cadences that operate in the two languages in a new way. The second point is about the lack of upper-case and punctuation in the German of *verlangsamte raserei*. The tradition of moving away from upper-case for nouns in German has its own particular logic for modern poets and a particular (also political) history. It allows for a less hierarchical sense to the poems in that nouns are not privileged above other grammatical units. It also allows multiple meanings to be exploited: a word might be simultaneously read as a noun or as a verb, or hover between them. Punctuation is also controlled by grammar to a much greater degree in German than in English. Reducing it to a bare minimum (often flying in the face of conventional grammar) contributes to that same sense of democratisation as the consistent use of lower-case; again allowing the line greater syntactic flexibility and opening up multiple readings. Both of these features are essential aspects of the feeling of lightness, indeterminacy, even whimsy, in Schlag's German. Especially in the more recent poems this is part of a concerted resistance to acceleration ('racing in slo-mo' is the programmatic title of the 2014 collection). One has to read slowly and carefully. Then one has to read again. However, the question about how to render this into English is more tricky. Certainly, all my early drafts followed this same path. But German grammar of itself does a good deal more scaffolding work than English. Over the course of long discussions the sense emerged that removing punctuation and upper-case in English would leave the language more, perhaps too, adrift; would distract from the work going on in the language itself; and might ally the poems with traditions and positions in the Anglo-American poetry scene that it simply does not share. I hope nevertheless that that distinctive lightness of touch, strangeness and the fluidity have been preserved in other ways in the English: 'Thoughtsnow Drifting'.

I have been supported during work on this project by New College, Oxford and the university's Faculty of Modern Languages in numerous ways, including bringing Evelyn Schlag to Oxford for a reading in 2007. Thanks are also due to The University of Innsbruck and New College, Oxford for financing a trip to Austria that allowed me to see Evelyn in her own environment and allowed us to work together intensively on the final drafts.

Karen Leeder
Oxford, May 2017

FROM

Sprache von einem anderen Holz

LANGUAGE OF A DIFFERENT STRIPE

2008

Portrait of Cecilia Gallerani
(Lady with the Ermine)

Everyone who sees her – even if it is too late
to see her alive – will say: that suffices for us
to know what is nature and what is art.

Bernardo Bellincioni

Where the road divides 72 km along the B121
I was filling up. Couldn't stop looking over.
She was so – well – she just turned you on.
You gawp – and petrol drips on your trousers.

Making for another planet. Nothing would turn
her head. Ramrod straight she stood there
as if waiting for that special someone
who didn't yet exist. She wore her brown hair

flat on her head like a scarf. These girls always
dress too skimpily. T-Shirt with a risqué scooped-
out neck and frilly arms. Little black necklace
tight round her throat. I thought: is that a tattoo?

On her arm – it took a while before I understood
it wasn't a bag or a scarf – she held a white beast.
I crossed over to the other side to look.
Head too small for a cat. Stuff of make-believe –

an ermine. Ages I stood there mouth open wide:
how still she was and the animal as well.
Won't something like that squirm? Piss and bite
and claw? The paw – hanging in front – to signal

stop! The creature smarter than the fragile thing
that stroked its neck. Perhaps a few bars
of the Balkan Blues on a loop in her head going
round. Or stoned enough to forget who she was.

A runaway. One never knows the violent
fathers oneself. Only trusted witness to it all
– it makes me weep – the wretched ermine.
Neither of them enough to tip the scales.

Nafea Faa Ipoipo (When Will You Marry?)

Gauguin should have been his painter. He knows
the family histories of the brightly coloured girls.

Today they have such large souls again
and their mothers invite him to stay.

Embrace. All of it was what I liked best.
I am pale up to the edges of the iodine.

European Colonies 8

Time out for the patients in casual clothes.
But it's not free time. It's ordinary daywear
and they're allowed to get dirty.

The woman's in tears because she can't
manage the step. Sobs bitterly inside
her hard helmet: a dripping pan reinforced

behind for the floating brain within.
Fastened under the chin with ears free.
She cries angrily and bares her teeth.

A young woman leads her by the hand
whose body is wise and eligible and tonight.
And her hair is not disabled nor her mouth.

She walks beside her hand in hand.
Blessed with her lucky genes she flies with
every step. Come on up you go – bitterly.

Under the sports-helmet of a crash-discipline
the woman conquers the step. The walk can begin.
It is early summer in the whiteboat harbour of the town.

She polishes the pavement with her shuffling steps.
The earth's surface underfoot the culture of marble.
Still she is mobile. Can still be pulled along.

A seagull in flight democratically shits itself free.
White snot between the stays of the helmet.
The masts of the boats find that unnerving

such strange turns of fate.

European Colonies 9

Wind that knows how to play with little children.
Water that kidnaps the folded paper boats and
pretends they will wash up on a little coast

where they will quickly dry and found a flotilla
or sit on a window-ledge as some exotic flotsam
from Europe along with a handful of stones.

A day with no breaking news and no deadly
wave. No minimum death tolls on stretchers.
No flickering figures at night tipped out

of boats into the hygienic hands of the coast.
Only flip-flops on the European waterfronts.
Oversized beach towels folded over their arms.

Hesitant Prospect

1

I love each and every finger on your hand
I'm sitting in the din behind the waterfall
ultra-sounded palace hazarded hearing
what do you want to know? I've followed
my paddle up the creek a way that's all
asphalt poetry in a Belarussian village
perhaps the only pose that's true

2

On the way down the steep slope there were
cars overtaking us all of them new this year
shining and not only with rain
                              clear outlines
finger on the tap a word and
                              they would tip
us into the ditch or even simply
off course and out of the grooves that ran
the length of the torn road down which
a huge hand had drawn an iron comb

We drove out across the hills past the expanse
of new-mown meadows in a rain growing
ever finer a rain chased towards us
by the sun
              The sun hung suspended in each one
of the millions of droplets so that we drove into
a wall that seemed to retreat and renew itself
as if we were driving through someone else's life
a life fulfilled complete in every way
a life in a wet and dancing light

3

A first image that rose above our horizons
no question the blazing plasma
of a human being just like us no question

Or were we the ones drifting beyond the here and now
because the temptation of light exceeded all we were.
Our whole life long other people die
are dressed and asked: is there anything you need?
No reply

Their way with words that we adored
their precious vocabularies that they take
to the grave in the pockets of their coats

4

Nature had altered its state and the co-ordinates
of physics relaxed their grip across the terrain
perhaps we were discharged at our own risk

We came out sideways from the sun onto a path
language of a different stripe
                              but you with me
in the rear-view mirror I saw that we were still on track
a tangle of caresses exuded in a fever of hearing

5

There was the field of maize each green-leaf at the ready
there was a plump young man chasing his dog
up across the meadow under a half-read
copy of the *Rainbow*
                              a twin-sky with make-up
we tried not to explain it to ourselves and besides
I no longer recall a single word from then but you

6

Formalised desire
buzzard and buzzard
they intimate
the distances to one another
correcting themselves as they fly
let it never end
swelling seam
we search for a new contour

7

Nothing in need of an *and*
I cannot speak for you
even if your breath
does cartwheels through my body

8

Unconsecrated meat green and blue and the T
of the spade-handle it is a feeling:
meeting the unawares
a wandering central strip
dated error
as if lifted from logic

9

How they coasted down in neutral behind you
screeching darkly only on the turn
one / the same one
flight helmet for a spin-second
pitched headover you and your shoulder

The lines of shaved thistles separate
as if I were tearing a sheet
in August I wash your armpits cursing
practise the clasps of the gentle corset
that embraces you from behind like a man

10

Seen from this far away all people
are made for one another
we wanted the shelter of interpretation
I can't hold out any longer
or hold myself back any more I can't
promise mouth to mouth

11

You have redeemed me you tell me unbelieving
it was only the way I like to be
in the air the thickening red of cloth and black
absolute vowels how you shake me or greet me
uncounted how you lose track of my absence
and kiss me in front of the cathedral wherever we go

12

Hesitant prospect
slowly stretches further
gives itself over to the near
the world I am writing into being
transforms itself into the *how*

Nordstau Effect

The play of light in the leaves
dapples your back. In draft it was
darker round us a sparing use of sun.

We were people without seasons on our heads.
An idea perfected in a tunnel is how we
seemed. Longing for contour and not a clue

that we'd become more modern. Ever
younger. Play of light your back. In pictures
the sails are patched with outstretched

arms the sun shines down on the heads
of the rowers. A woman shields her eyes
with her bare forearm her mouth is scarcely

more than three dots. When I'm cold you fetch
me into the house warm-blooded creature you
alter my pulse. Your voice is even. You explain

the sudden snow the fading northern light
the pirates on the weak grey sea the nerve under
my eye that makes my gaze seem fixed in

a way I'd never want to be in face of your love

Where Our Skin

Before autumn we had not given ourselves to each other.
Each of us turning our red foliage into the southernmost
corner of North. Secretly you slip me an extra leaf.

In winter we will again believe that it's us who are
getting smaller. It's the sun leaning back on its
haunches. It's the beast that must find us.

I ask myself when it was that the settlers' mountains
soaked up the names of new arrivals with such ease.
Your elegant nose. Now we know one another

by our underarms where our skin is not ashamed.

Bodies Well Lost

Even as autumn keeps its distance
I will imagine for you the little teeth of the ivy
and here the kiss of the blossom in my hand.

So many things cast out again from the year
shovelling with both arms letting each day
end without saying: you can't count on us!

Grandiose storms follow on behind the time.
If you glance to the side there are outlets
with three flags all the zones one needs.

The snow will be washable at least
a menu for the disabled. What I need:
desert. Casino signs of the Cree and the Sioux.

Where there's nothing there are trading grounds
for sale. The selling fields. Fields. The highest
secular building was the cooperative silo.

At night we take one another's hands it happens
in a courtly way and we know our bodies are well lost
in the form of sleep the biographical head released

from the scree of running images

We Did Not Carry

Our closest kin is winter.
We stand behind on tip toes.
Before we realised they'd packed up

everything we owned their precision
scrapers pivot lamps where we froze
without a clue. The sun keeps shining

into late November. Every day
a little more at home. Last yellow leaves
flutter past under the dog's belly.

And every phrase hangs exposed in the air.
Absence hurts from wherever you are.
Come winter our thoughts will be seen.

We did not carry any weight

Shukran Dimashq

Soon the slopes will don the robe of light and rest their
heads to sleep. Beyond them the logical Anti-Lebanon
that we will see only when we wake. The notebooks

coated in green plastic like our teachers used to have.
You will know nothing but the shape of the mountain.
We do one another secret services. Wait in the souk

at the appointed times. No one sticks to the plan.
We too are growing careless about our futures.
We thought you were ahead but you were far behind.

Your mouth is stuffed with a nightingale nest. Your speech
is honey nest you say pistachio instead of piaster.
Black ostrich feathers scattering the dust on limousines.

Sufi and Versailles. Gateway to fresh-squeezed apple juice.
Police direct the traffic somewhat with a scarf and cigarette.
At night little sledges career across the roofs.

Santa Claus hangs unharmed in the Christian quarter

St Petersburg Poem: The Truth

I never forget that you are a man. Even when you
quote me for lines on end. Down the Griboyedov
up Nevsky Prospect in the golden September shadow.
That's what you're built for – long conversations not
small talk. We hold forth across your squares.

You call me broad female person. You lay your
Moyka round my shoulders. Your fish nibble at
my neck hairs – how come we are not serious?
Your every column both argument and ornament.
Your veto on stone for other cities smacks of envy.

You show me all these empty plastic bottles. No
messages. No reader conjured for a time to come.
One of these bottles took to sea and came ashore
at Komarovo. Decoration for her grave. A single
long-stemmed white lily. You would like it. A wall.

Only watering cans and faded rubbish lacking.
The letters of her name are cut too shallow
in the stone. The needles from her trees can't
sink down and read her like other trees read
their dead poets – readers transposed by the

wind in a library. Can you hear how cold I am.
You are not my first city – just the first freezing one
that deigns to smile. We pass through one another.
I press five leaves into your hand. Suddenly
it comes to me how beguiled by needles I am.

Whoever gets too close to you (like this young
sky) can only blame themselves when they bleed.
The islands are already onto it and flinch away in pain.
Seeing you like this the many windows of your beauty.
You – a gambler. How I believed your black night.

Always telling each other life stories – right?
You are so dreadful. Go on try the fish.
Names bandied back and forth. Sometimes
the reflections drift away in all directions.
Now I know what you mean. Most imaginary city!

Genealogy News

Surrounded by adjustable headthistles picking
up the Saturday news: leaves behind his
parents and a brother. Oldest of seven children

and signed up of his own free will. The morning
was still cooler than a cheek. Chairs on the veranda.
Outside the tiny dolls' hands seem to sweat.

Also leaves behind his parents. Smart exit
the little garden gate falls to behind the lost
son. When he's back he'll get round to mending it

and leaves behind his parents and two sisters.
Petrol station and new potatoes. The noises join
forces head for happiness. This photo leaves behind

his parents and two brothers. A laundry ticket
means nothing at all. Green garden wire rolled up
next to the shears. Listening out for the one name

and leaves behind his parents two brothers and a sister.
Free-floating fatherhoods disappear in the Holy Scripture.
In the madness of initials: who was who in the male line

and even then the bloggers meddle in what came after

Lost Gardens of Heligan

First it becomes a sanatorium for soldiers
shell-shocked amidst well-meant experiments.
Each man's soul housed in two museums.

No image comes back not a step from the
jungle bridges even the virtual tour brings
nothing from a world that once breathed.

At night the overbooked studio of my sleep.
In my confusion I lost the gardens even
though they took me in like paradise.

Waist-high in the garden of ... fragment of silk
or was it dishonoured tweed surely it is enough
to speak to lay down a store of new recollections

outside of memory which anyway lied or
threw away its uniform in Heligan as it ran
down the last slopes in pure colour!

*Sweep*sound

5

Should I bring you my body language? Now?
Today we still haven't told each other doggy
stories but they can wait. Of the eight hundred
hands that pain me every day you maybe use
a dozen. I practice gymnastics to reach towards
the gods. Standing helpless before the sketches.
Just come soon however unwatered you are.
And now my foot is counting whether you have
all your toes. Squirts of sperm and dug-outs of desire.
I'd like to have earned many more places: fetch me
from every side. Your breath is sweet again.
I would like to have been made out of your pleura.

We were much surrounded by the light
of glowing blossom. Weightless above our heads
like unwritten poems. They coloured a room
for us neck-shortened animals. But it was about
much more as I learnt in the marathons:
Life. Domestic life. I enlarged my breath
and you were still there. Soon you would be able
to take over my memory as far as over-fluff
is concerned. The original fluff of the literal.
For a time I had to go to the other side of the car
in order to explain who you are in your absence.

If Bohemia Lies by the Sea

OK Ingeborg: that's enough.
Last week on the English Isles I read out
four times that mighty hymn of yours.
No doubt the sea had moved to the North.
It was rocking on itself
and the allusions scurried back to their own century.
Two children kept running out of the water:
without a fever into February.

I let myself freeze wanted to see from the tower to the Tiber.
I'd been given a coin without currency
that vanished into the slit of a mouth.
Perhaps fetched in by a tongue.
One entered a cage with four chambers.
Iron bars tall as a man. A ribcage from the Middle Ages.
The turnstile jammed held me fast.
A prelude to death? A CIA trick?
In the grille of cold I accented you differently again.

Cassandra marching in pale step.
An unloved woman who sticks by her lines.
The carnivores hold onto their place amidst a cunning gender.
I even put my hand into the lion's mouth.
Should one let this kind of love pass by?
Strange insomnias arrive and stay the night.
We hadn't known how close we were coming to others
while seeking out room for manoeuvre.
Lions (yes lions) and abbeys where the roofs have flown away.

I can report: months are missing in every year.
I scream into my hands a good deal. Am not guilty of any
audience.
What my eyes see: at the edge of the woods
a slender raised hide has snagged a tree.
Weighed down by its oversized head the killing pulpit.

My eyes see photos:
skeletons of two lovers from thousands of years ago.
Their embrace is still intact.

News of the day is the little lollipop feet
of the premature baby of 22 weeks
that – if one took them in the mouth as crazy lovers sometimes do –
would melt there.
Jelly lozenges almost translucent.

My eyes saw your eyes where they live on.
In glances before language.
In features that preserve your genes.
We know less than ever before.
The seas run over to their friends reach as far as

all that ever was Bohemia. All that ever lay on no coast.

No Pathos Please

1

I should let them go the wolves
that are gnawing at my wrist.
In January they tear open the embrace
and a delta of pain burns in the snow.
My voice grows quiet with the howling
the first wolf takes language on a detour:
I love you with your skin your hair.

2

The place we go to fetch our later years
is always in season. The sponge brushes
noiselessly over the undipped paper.
What shall I call you when it's winter
and your soul storms at the window?
In spring when your sorrow falls down into
the valley as snow? We live a thousand times.

3

Pushed on the trolley like this under the lights.
Whoever we are our height is tilted
our name is written on a white wrist band.
When I am back amongst the figures
I'll write to you without greenery only with
blossom and my liberated hand. It will not get me.

4

I went into this sleep with half a phrase
on my lips and awoke with a silence.
It is cold.
                Someone pulls a blanket
over my naked undecorated shoulder.
I've grazed out in the cosmos – stomach and head

are empty. A piece of me is missing and more.
How will I find my way back from here to my law?

5

Safe in the flood of your thoughts
I didn't have to face what I knew.
No alphabet inscribed in me I was
laid out in white instead of black the way
you like me. I lay in my own forgetting.
All that's left is the aesthetic of a cut
curved and fine as a hair – when will your
names return? Faith and refuge and always
a third thing: that's what you gave me.

6

Climbed out of the panic pod where
I'd made my home hands folded above
my head. My throat scratched by the tube.
A few words have been destroyed.
                              This morning I heard
an angel. She always breathed out all
her breath. She said: see how you ensnare
me. I want to make a path for you
when the temperatures start to fall.
That was in my Finnish days in a tongue
quite different from Finnish. From you.

7

I know I've woken up wrong again.
The night's still busy laying its sex
here and there and the writing
has not returned to the whitewashed wall.
No one taking charge no one calls the shots.
Poets are named after the living dead.

8

Sometimes the wound cavity fills up
with the clear streaks of conversation.
Someone has thanked me for a black kite
and my engrossed face. He didn't want
to lose me just to slip me into the day
before like an addiction. Library of the
weaned – *without limits you are wonderful.*

Conditio Divina

1

You exchanged us under false pretences.
If anyone ever gets to the bottom
of your secret language they will not
know what to say to you. You have taken
no responsibility for this work of yours that gives
us pain. You don't even have a name.
You've invented every illness so that we
lose our composure at night. No one holds
us safely in balance nor ever balances us out.

2

Nothing sticks to you. Your conscience slides
like seawater from your feathers. You let us go
too soon after just a moment of suspicion.
You've worked until the point of exhaustion and
lost your patience with us so fast. Head on one side.
You know: of all the dying birds none will be
saved. Even the Holy Spirit will be culled.
We long for the bright green that turns our
heads. The truth is that we left. You standing there.

3

In fact you should idolize us – we who go
along with all your games. Idolize us instead
of making us guilty with a man who cheats the grave.
You've trotted out all these children's stories
and required us to believe. Consoled us
like a sadist. Given short shrift with the bursting
promise of a blue yonder always beyond our grasp.
All the time we whimper from the radiation doses.

4

As if there had ever been anything you didn't
know with that omniscience of yours. As if free
will had ever been a choice for us. As if it had not
been you who chose him for the terrible task
ahead. Made his mother lose her mind.
As if we with our inherited guilt had not
given the call for his death. As if we needed
empty graves and circus tricks. As if we hadn't
had more than enough of your hubris long ago.

5

Gentle Lord: the signs were everywhere
in the fields and gave us warning. The earth
was infested with your plagues but
as always you were in the clear.
We bore the death warrants of beasts on our soles
and could not come up with yours. The list
of farms gone to ruin gets longer every day.
A sheep and cattle farm at Abergavenny.
A sheep and cattle farm at Bodorgan.
Three cattle and sheep farms at Welshpool.
Wet houses of stone remained. The horizons
were obscured with flames. The gripper hands
of diggers took hold between ribs and horns.

6

It's not as if we didn't sometimes sense
you clearing your throat. When you start
defending yourself and there's no word left
for your disgrace. No phrase to account for your guilt.
You would have to revoke the world in order
to understand what we are about: struck
blind. Only whale song in our deaf ear.
You've never felt anything first hand.
We all have only this one body.

7

This is how it might have been. Afternoon.
Everything already in place: intelligent mounds of grass.
Militia in white camouflage against the corrugated
desert. Their name in italics and gorgeously sexy.
That afternoon you wanted to create something
lasting – a mortal life – but that already existed.
Everything existed already. This time you wanted
to do your very best but were uncertain
of the genre. You were so sad not to have been
made of flesh. Fallen flat and unwanted
the chromosomal event on the West Bank.

8

Background quietly exploding away.
A double helix awakes with a greater than
human deficit. Some afflictions are suprahuman.
What else would there be to say? However well
he can dance when sitting: hands moving
above his head someone is struggling to make sense.
Music only needs to be music. Green green.
What else is there to say in the inextinguishable
urge to address surrounded by evolution
alias God: we're waiting for your *I'm desperate.*

All under One Roof

I think of this as a mutable monster that
takes a deep gulp and all the micro-names
– that's us – are sucked in at the entrance.

Interior lighting in a globogob. Tongulator
to the first floor. Not looking no one in the
eye. Sinking faces long since swilled away. Not

in the market for friends. Nameless plankton the
lot of them shopperplankton drifting. The season's
innocent colours have arrived like never before.

Swallowed in the mawstrom check-in at the gills.
So much identity overheard in the changing rooms.
Yet another relationship falling apart. Will you come

later will you come on after me I want you to come.
Indoors you mean or on the shopping trail? Dunno.
No idea what you're on about. Shopping world?

I've got crushed silk not the real stuff. The kosher
sort's what grows on roadside trees know what
I mean on bushes just like grubs. Falls to the ground

like in spring. When it's Japan. Not China

Downfall Blues

Along the coastline the carcasses of freight ships.
Burst containers that couldn't face the swell
spewing motorbikes and disposable nappies.

The old instincts for plunder always kick in.
Anything portable is carted off by the kids
and civic duty turns up too late to the party.

If no owner makes themselves known we will   .
acquire a taste for the product personality. Happy
waves. After the purchase comes the slump.

We should have taken a few hip-joints with us.
Perhaps we can exchange goodbyes or hold
our hair between the scissor blades. Honestly:

I want to hold my hair between the scissor blades

Sense of Time

The daytime here lasts from six AM till five.
The old fliers reach the very edge of their
exhaustion. They stop and rub their eyes

before the day begins in allergies and trips.
The word that held a world of promise
for the diva: I lived it in a micro-sleep.

Now people everywhere all stay awake
updating their newest curriculum vitae
in broad nightlight and smogdark days.

I no longer take much notice of the night
since it's started stretching out its hours.
I wait in the twilight between what's thought

and done and our words are never really ours.

FROM

verlangsamte raserei
RACING IN SLO-MO

2014

Plaits

1

My first plait was the hair of fairy tales.
I was not yet brunette and thought in blond.

I dreamed of princes wrote the sample letter
for a secret. When I swallowed what they

said I sometimes closed my eyes. My feet
in lace-up shoes my wrist too delicate.

A head for heights and never broke my heart.
Thorn thorn be thou my scorn. But when the

chequered boys came ringing on my plait it was
the moment for mutilation. They grasped at nothing.

2

The second plait hung from the window into
the stream. Water wound it round the stones.

I hauled it out with blazing stars and wiped
my hands across my apron. Painted thawing

winter meadows with its brush-tip. Green
strands of hair helped and I was filled

with longing for the sea. I yearned to fetch
ten mussels and weave them into spring.

3

The third plait did not mix so well. It hung
down from my neck just like a tail. Giraffe or

ostrich. I stood by the garden fence and heard
the ting ting ting: the barriers coming down.

Song of the rails and goods trains rattling past.
Chalk figures chalk signs on the rusty

metal. If I stared at wheels they started
turning backwards. Under fir trees comfort.

4

The fourth plait found its own way to me –
a sudden extra weight with tiny golden beads

sticks of cinnamon and scent of laces.
Gift between my shoulder blades – true virtue.

I was caught up with growing. Saw the
women on their way to tailored dresses

with their hourglass waists cast off. My
youth was now so far away in spite of

giant steps. My steps: protruding knees
flat heels unladylike and ultra-pale.

5

The last plait a deserter now unbuttoned.
Sudden children chased me in the setting sun.

I heard their footsteps on the side and up above
but they couldn't catch me. I so wanted to

stand still and watch a dog with wet paws slurping
water. It was easy. The swaying at my neck swung

towards the eighth of May: they reached the River
Enns with tanks and full equipment. A splash

and war just fell away. The girls woke up with legs.
Head-turner. Loose boards. Stones for fear. Rage.

Girl's Room

In the mid-nineteen-sixties I knew
the capital city of Liverpool spent
long nights lost in the fever
                    of fandom

and went on scratching this spot
raw. On the walls the distant face
of my father and the treble he
                    probably heard.

When others began heavy petting
I scratched and rinsed the blood from
my pyjamas. Sugar itching under
                    my nails.

Bad jokes about an old bloke *clock
the bees humming round his flies*
and anyway who condemned me
                    to this spot

where such ill-fated pathways met?
Diabetes Beatles – bloody eunuchs
my father'd say – and at night I scratched
                    the itch to death.

Souvenir

Foreign benediction over my parents' bed the
red and gold icon from father's Russian war
it lay there on the dung-heap at the farm
                    would only have rotted

empty gestures limbs stumps an inside view
of scraps of ideas only insides only outsides
then a decision for the supreme discipline
                    of red surgery

he was still at the local hospital when his first
reattached hand sent him holiday greetings
                    written like a ghost.

Hospital in Those Days

Novalis Novartis all the sisters the same
with their lives set aside their narrowed
faces their hands blue from indulgences.

They say: let's not beat about the altar
there's no job here for our lover
any more. They kneel before the tabernacle.

Host wafers crunch. Novalis calls it secret
love in the glove compartment God knows
why. Novartis whispers: you must upgrade

into chronic. Cornflowers bluebells all things
blue come in at our door. We have hold
of you under your arms. Die or blossom!

Novalis drums a cross with hard knuckles
on her forehead collarbone and breast.
Prayer fists of a kangaroo says Novartis.

Up in the theatre things are more worldly.
The services of both unpaid like the morning.
In this life orders barked from behind the mask.

The man in white stands there and is all eyes.

Indigo

I dream of indigo the way it used to be.
Outline of the blueberry patch. Mosses
fleeing the chalk and we had a word.

Wilma fled school. Karina meat.
We layered pine needles on top. Each
one carrying our little idols to the woods

to burn. To burn. My indigo would not
burn and I stayed on the outside. Lips
when one weeps. A trembling chin. It would

never be mended. My indigo could speak
and had its place in the basin at night.
I whispered and sang along with it in a

high voice. It was no one's fault. Next year
the romantic countries will come over
to our side. Into the gloom. Into the blue of walls.

Thoughtsnow Drifting

from the west. Brings with it the idea of time.
The birds sitting all fat and puffed up on the
balcony: yellow-bellied red-capped. Blackbirds
      in charge at the feeding station.
Rotten trees on the mountain slowly falling

to their deaths. March is hard to survive. A dopey
pair of doves falls in love above the branch
peers over at the satellite dishes and chooses
      as always a lifelong marriage.
When will it be the Tuesday after winter?

In the cellars monologues run out of steam.
Love letters make no headway at all.
The detail is in the ink. In freehand he wrote
      for ages I've wanted to write to ...
and went into the dark wood. The days are still

short the nights are getting shorter. *Wanted to*
write once more ... listening for the call of life
from those days. All of it from those days. Quiet
      presses on your face. How
did we look at each other? How did our bodies lie?

Thoughtsnow drifting from the west through the hour.
Stretches the oversize of waiting. *Want never*
to see you again winter all flaked off.
      The zizibe we thought was old
the three-second-sweetness on replay is here.

Déserteur D'amour

You were up and gone no sign-language could
hold you. You wanted to mean nothing any
more. A draught between a cold back and
       comfort. I called after you: *say*
tomorrow at five. Just say tomorrow. At five.

Unknown episodes come to light as soon
as I speak to the projectionist. A hand held
into shot with a boxed ear running from it:
       recipient unknown.
Often you'd been capable of anything.

Sound man with such wonderful effects.
I can't get it out of my ears the way you
moaned round my head howled into my mouth
       only you only me only
who? Splish-splash nights. Tea at eight.

Lady of Montana on the Rein

For a long time it was circles by the fence.
The mare was called *My Lady of Montana*
and seemed to like her name.
          You of course were crazy
for the myth of it her tender parts.

An arm appears around your shoulder as soon as
you've dismounted. Keeps your neck from feeling
chilly. Ironed fabric and every seam just so.
          The smell of roof ridge
under many suns asked you: is that

perhaps a saddle partner? Spurs on his boots
like the little wheel in the kitchen that draws
a perfect line through the dough.
          Sing along to this as well.
To the harmonica and the cowboy beer.

Better in front of the shutters than
wasting the rosiness in a pale light.
Languishing ahh and looking past
          his bad finger joints:
if he's a man with a monogram

take him. Handkerchiefs and no more.
There's his age. When his lasso falls from his
hand then it will be time. For different stitching
          and a modern material
that dries without creases in a lady-friendly way.

Random Man

In the Euro tunnel on the great west track
the glasses tremble on the table. I think of bats
and their tiny spit. For sticking speech marks
          back when they've fallen off
quotations. It's fine it's fine. The little witches

are growing fingernails. It's fine it's fine. Far
away they play the harpsichord. As soon as day
breaks our random man appears. Looks like your
          lost lover in the shape
of his eyes eyelids: you dole out a little

silver chain. Are we at square one again?
Will he know? Take your ankle by surprise
and emerge a gentleman from such depths?
          Whisky moon it's fine it's fine.
You cling to equilibrium like blackbirds

with a head for heights. Wheels rolling. You
want to talk about roof terraces and it's fine.
It's fine. You share the same favourite
          lines from 'Family Strife in
Hapsburg'. Snowlaughter. Fingertip.

On the Rocks

Water-skater my green-limbed friend
who invites me down to breakfast.
I know his cheek his stubby
          beard but most of all
his books. Intimate updates read

breath by breath judged and forgotten.
In times when we're ignored we egg each
other on. Feel like elves toeing on the
          tips of our tongues.
In his case it's a feature film.

From page to page the two of us a
mirror image. The sounds of running
get closer to the heart of the eclipse
          where I froze in the void:
great thought vanished without trace.

Then more water-greetings and savouring
the air then fish-in-the-river without a care.
It's the same for him as me. We stay just
          friends inches above
our hands and everybody knows the score.

Olga

Checks in under Helga. Real name is
Olga. Had a youth like any other. Broken
love lies scattered about. Not a good start
       but there'll always be cat litter
if you want to have clean streets.

A few one-to-ones with the boss. She hangs
grey trousers without creases measures
blood pressure to order. After that looks for
       tiniest mislaid shirt buttons.
The cute guys think of her as a private

TV flesh and hair 3D something like
tip-top totty totally trippy all in triplicate. Speedy
German. Comes from a village in the East
       that's on its last legs. Her mother
never showed her how to live with a view.

Strange things sometimes happen in Olga's passport.
When asked about her dream job she confesses
window cleaner. Eye to eye with
       airspace that's still swaying.
And before her breathed-out fears of strangers.

High-rise I. Vulnerable only to technical
faults or lightning strikes and swarms
of birds drunk on the wind collectively
       lost in a demo-loop.
Not even coming down to earth in search of prey.

Unarmed Civilian Security Service

The CCTV camera bears witness to the
little town hyenas or perhaps this willingness
to commit violence is the product:
      a girl of about fifteen
strikes and grapples with a rival pulls and kicks

her six times as she's already crumpled on the
deck. There's often trouble at this stop. Yellow
jackets full of security surround the scene
      stand by. Their contract vetoes
any kind of intervention. Gang members quickly

duck and pick up ipod mobile handbag
collateral gains. For sure the victim is no sweet-
heart. No one is a sweetheart. Perhaps the
      littlest girl with her silver jacket
who stands looking at the kicked-in skull then

skips away her school bag bobbing up and down.

Charmeur

A rush of recognition – lifts me without effort
to your gaze. The solid background with
an eyelash kiss. Then you embrace me
      hardly leaving room for rosemary
or bag. Your face reveals a sudden flash

of how oblique the day is: slanted like a flight
of steps into the sideheart of the city. We almost
lose our footing in this stupid floating:

what were you about
to say? *Next week we will be up to our necks*

in Marrakesh and you? It's all just a distraction.
And if it has to be then let's choose Casablanca.
You have time at all for me? My inner
      working's on the blink
again. The car door grabs my glove.

So tell me how should I stay calm when
you just can't stop playing old school
in that crazy German – and me so
      hyper-hectic in between
a sandwich and the super power USA.

Cirrus

or circus clouds. A school of flying
dolphins standing still a while in such
a sky at ten to twelve. From you? They
      drift apart – too many flakes
that make your message undecipherable.

I pull up periwinkle in my garden wicked
ivy binds adventures to the ground.
It puts its finger on escape attempts:
      with all its piano-claws
so one leaf gives the next and you embrace

me like old England's time. A repeat-spring
strikes the heart a repeat bird-call. This
is where the tulip bulbs were dug up:
      what do you make of that?
If it was Tiger you'll have to forgive him.

Études

In the lectures our handwriting wrote itself
into a new character. We had blood
      on our fingers and sat
          near Romanticism.

The muscle twitch in our forearms looked the part.
Did he say Keats did he say Shelley drowned
      and passing lightly over
          the Spanish flu.

We were reading true to life en route to shared
apartments. Lent each other our hands.
      Bit by bit a certain style emerged
          around the mouth

and the fingers as we smoked: which film
did you steal that from or is it all your own?
      A dramaturgy developed and
          private semesters.

And that's how you fitted into the decade and how
I was how you were: love coming into being
      on a hot red face. Breathing broken
          word for word

Season before Half past Ten

Scarcely stumbled from the train and
struggled to my feet I see you
waving with your glove hands. It all

bends towards your sign and turns away.
Hands of your watch close round me:
you are as always bigger. Snow is

flying at your brow. Your cheeks are red
your eyes against the wind. We treat ourselves
to an adventure a real old-fashioned one

and round our legs the sombre loneliness
of tiger stripes. No one looks my body
up and down. No one swims so quietly

through the night. A man mislays his book
en route. Sevastopol you're on your knees.
Kriemhild? Criminal? It sounds like Easter bells

Coronary CT

Primary colour: alert but with iodine.
You have pulsed your way back down to calm.
  In your thorax the arrival
of the contrast *but I still know*

that last day and you hear distorted
echoes of instructions in urgent tones.
  With a sweet-smelling mouth…
you drift in the depths of memory while

a non-invasive interest seeks out
a billion bits of data per second.
  In the blink of an eye
your whole inner-life exposed. World of zeros

where you were the hero. The image of all
you ever wanted becomes a positive finding.
  But I can still remember
how your arm around me is dissolved in

local spatial dimensions in millimeasures.
But it's not your head your brain it's just
  a replaceable organ
you wait for and time stands still.

You are so individual and according to age.
Half-lines squabble for your meaning.
  Your mourning score is appreciably
reduced. Awaiting gnostic evaluation

Renaissance Song

for Friederike Mayröcker

I bring you greetings from a mate who's
often seen his name in your book of late:
John Dowland like download the ladies
sitting pretty download his dittys. Lute music.

The hoarfrost on his voice has turned to
dew. While he says semper dolens of himself
the mood not so much highland as Holland
and the lyrical ladies at court are alight.

Sweet sound a word too loud for his soul
that laces the lovelands like fog. Lets you know
there must be decades of books to applaud
reliable surprises clouds of floating dust.

Met him on the *islands* insects of arrival
on my brow. Lets you know the boiling
streets of his youth were brimful of tears
but that made the world different and clear.

Wind Song

In the wind you turn
your ear to understand
your beloved and speak
inside out for a dog's sake.

Freezing northsides. And we
shall have snow. Soon your
whole body will know: will
turn sullen like the wind.

Suddenly you're all thumbs
and only have half a profile:
wind in the flight-village when
the cows see us from above.

Ancient oaths and cloudleaps
stand before you: promised
like words on the wind. No bird
no hail vying to be saved.

In the wind you turn yourself
inside out for a dog's sake
and speak with your ear to
understand your beloved.

Poor Russia Song

Bodies bodies kidney shield.
Tiny arms of dolls tacked on.
Squaddies splitting Georgian skulls.
The widow Chadorkovskaya.

Bodies bodies soft as ground.
Red blood on Evil Square.
A slender shoulder out of joint.
The corpse of Politkovskaya.

Little Afternoons

In my head there's always din as soon as
I want peace. The parties put to bed I want
to sit in trees. Bounding down (a little hare)

would be the way to do it. In the arms of some
brill-creamed dreamboat who is this week's
squeeze. But speaking in the open I can't see

my issues any more: peace. Peace would be
a different life. Peace was a day or two
between home cooking baby food and then

I simply licked the pattern off the plate.
I need a blanket for my shoulders. Jenny
was so cute in white velour not like her

parents in their autumn camouflage. Or Jürg
with built-in kitchen and the milk is boiling
over. Not so much the fags as all of us were

smokers then. All. Never had a bloke that
didn't smoke. One guy could play the cello
that was way too deep for me. Dangerous.

Market Day

I have given Kasimir an advent wreath
for his mother. In these sudden winters
dedications are worth more than pretty poetry.

Herta is there (with her cardinal red cheeks)
and the frequent daughters from the bakery.
At the butcher's van they buy tickets

for the alligator show. A tattooed haunch
of venison walks along at Heidi's side.
Soon Kasimir will spend eight weeks with

mangos. Will hold his hands into the sun.

Schengen Area

Pottered over from Slovakia to Poland
just like that. They remember collecting

countries and stamps with seabirds and
cans of lumpfish caviar any written scrap.

Outside a marten scurries over the car. Bikes
found two streets further on. Everything

on the move these are moments of political joy
you must lay down in your coronary arteries.

I want to know that I'm asleep not dream
that I'm awake. Such floodlit clearings.

Sleeping through in this new continent
its rocky plains. No shadows everything

wrapped clear and concrete in the need to look
with eyes closed. We should be laughing

anonymous tears at the borders fallen
so hard. Jam today – oh yes José. The fences

soon will be a fairy tale like Vietnam and
that sweet Snow White.

Ukraine

Poverty steeped in mud it cannot be says
someone to Natasha who should know.
          Sorting stock in the supermarket

in pink waistcoats bits of work about the house.
Flies off the shelves. Doesn't say: piece of work.
          Doesn't say: flies off

over the men itself. How do you mean
what self? Suddenly a hope squeaks
          into the local salesman's checklist.

Grown into the tables fleshed out into the
purest foam of girl on the cappuccino.
          Natasha reads the signs

on service stations toilets and the nameplates
in the field. In the hollowed scrap of concrete sky
          she glimpses a distant image of her

dignity. Girls with heels women with hard faces.

Predetermined Breaking Point

From fifteen it's always your fault what with
parents who will never pay enough attention.
Whether the cellar lights are on and other flowers.

It's about those different sums I tell you. Running
rampage through the beds and who will pay the bill?
My throat's a little ouchy with those windows

you capeesh? A hoarse-voiced late-shift in Diavolo.
I like myself when words come easy: splinter
is a stab in cushion-heart. The dislocated

child's arm bobbing in the bunk or you got
any questions? Every second Tuesday is
when bio-waste extends to murdered cats.

Reading problems? Cut the chit-chat please
and eaves are dropping from all sides. Drunk as
skunks. The old girl's got that wotsit GPS. The

only thing to save them would be eyes. A zone
like this of living asphalt. And before you knew it
there were parents not sure exactly when.

So why should I remember? No one can make me.
Shut your gob or else we'll drown in lingo.
My throat's a little ouchy and my jaw drops to the

grass. There'll be stupid blood here soon.

New York City Marathon

Good day to you Paula Radcliffe flying high.
With every step at the line in your mind.
A late autumn on fleeing soles. Asphalt

is the sky you tread with your feet.
Your white gloved hands (Minnie Mouse)
slice the seconds in two for that long

breath. Good day to you Paula Radcliffe born
in a blizzard. Your head throws every stride
over your shoulder for the one on your tail:

can she use it? And now into the final mile.
No time for what has slipped away. The men
would never have caught you not in eighty races

round the world. Good day Paula Radcliffe. I scan
for my brother's face at the side of the route.
Is he waving at me or at you? Your little baby takes

you in its arms.

Depression

*Slowly but surely the Atlantic depression in the form of ex-Helene,
the cyclone left behind after the tropical storm, moves further inland
and forces the high pressure front Leo into retreat.*

Ah ex-Helene you're my cyclone and so
    cruel. I'll be holding my hat for sure.
        Tears streaming from my eyes. That's

wind illness already in my face. I'm afraid
    of you in times like these: a dark cloud
        on the edge of my embroidered suns

and in the evenings you're already booked.
    Hold on. Breathe on me. What for? Because
        I need you for my notes and in the sand

the dog is digging for its rattle.
    I kept faith with you in the odd and in
        the even years. But don't think that's

the end of the name. Do you recall what you
    first thought of me: this guy eyes gummed
        with sleep this bloke and his vague lips

is meant to be a poet? I wanted you to see the town Tarifa.

Mobile Couple

A woman in a wheelchair and
the man cycling next to her
is pushing her – his hand on

her shoulder. Like in the country
of the young when every road
led to the cinema or into the sea!

White perms and flimsy scarves
– wheeling and fairdealing
on the tip of their tongues.

Seagulls and the touch of a finger
now the roles are reversed:
her motor pulls the bike along with

the man. He takes a breather does not
begrudge the silver one in her carriage
this lovely stretch of Brahms movement.

Passenger

The shore of the lake fades away as I forget
where we are. Houses flighthouses flee from me
along with the last cattle in the bend. Hub

called evening. Young man gets on the western
heaves his heavy suitcase in the rack:
I find myself eye to eye with an appendix

scar on a stranger's blond belly. Not half
sexy. Flashlight surface three seconds long.
A hair's breadth between me and farewell.

I did not shift a muscle from the spot
just shut my eyes at the very last moment.
Once I would have said very forbidden things.

High Water

Over there the cliffs the swallows' homes.
They shrug their shoulders at the rain.
River muscles the bawling floods.

This side of the Ybbs we see floating gardens
ducks done with surfing waddle along
the tarmac. No messing with them.

An aluminium ladder clinging to the house
with one hand. Not springing free it trampolines
between the water and the rush of its own weight.

Dug-outs cavorting in the roaring surge fringed
knights that – come their time – impale
themselves. One day we'll see the photos.

Sleeping Partner

Hanna lying on the slope sees the neurotransmitters
blowing by. The lightning gives. The lightning takes.

A gentle law governs these electrical discharges
like flowers sprouting along the neural pathways.

In principle creation makes sense and is green.
'Hallucinated Moldau' is the colour she'd call it.

Year by year the slow-release runs down. Impatience
alone hastens barefoot. Hanna lying on the slope with

an overdose of waiting. How many heaps of embroidery
how many welcomes postponed until the tardy hero

stumbles over the ridge of the hill. Dizziness.
In her mouth the dryness of the never-kissed

and always the greedy conventions lying in wait.

Economic Itineraries

1

In the East the logos of all the shiny new
companies. Soon the whole valley will be
    filled with the dreams of the jolly folk

and their casual poses. With the sound
of things bursting the threefold rattle
    of flags at the mall. The true insignia

of the town no longer signing the horizon. All
the halls illuminated at night. Even the xxs
    sizes occur in giant letters.

2

In the backlight from the disco outside
in a landscape like this: unprotected merchandise
    leans coughing as she smokes.

Girls girls standing swimming all along
the curve of revolution. Rain. This
    rage of their giant trucks.

The windscreen wipers have gone berserk and
inside a man clears the bar with the length
    of his arm. Something shatters.

So you've got it in your head after a great
thirst so you've got it. A line of poetry appears
    I wandered through the forest

of your hair. I wandered a lorry in camouflage: it
looks like the driver is clutching at his
    heart and *the forest of your hair.* Gets

out. Approaches. Is near. Feels up her
ambush and her hearing. Picked alive
        or snap-frozen? Swing load

embrace. Whimper on the ground. The
Eastern bloc has always merited our sympathy
        and today with gratitude we can:

support staff have remained for the most part
female. Pavements full to bursting with
        make up. Thighs not quite case-

hardened criss-crossed arms hugged tight to knees.
Very foolish patch-heart: in a flap. Cut to the chase
        like a punter's bypass. It goes bang!

About the Light (New York)

Joseph Mallord William Turner stayed out
in the storm for four hours bound to the mast
of the ship. Allowed his head to fill with the howl

of the wind around him and the fear of death.
A lady visiting the salon admired the painting.
Turner flew into a rage. No one had the right

to like this picture. He had seen the baleful
cheek of the moon as the deluge drew
itself up and the animals fled one way

the flight of birds another. Tell-tale
sign that the world was going under.
He painted avalanches waterfalls snowstorms

and Hannibal crossing the Alps. Which of these
tiny figures is Hannibal? Turner himself seemed
half-dead in the mountains. Change of

scene: in *Rain Steam and Speed – The
Great Western Railway* on the Maidenhead
Bridge. The narrow-set eyes of the train

racing towards you. A beast of prey
with the evil eye. So far so well-known.
But now let us imagine: William Turner

as night falls in Manhattan. The lights on all
the floors flicker on. What message is being
morsed? Dot dot pause dot dash – he wants

to catch that fraction of a second between dark
and light. Sees the stream of lines without meaning.
Sees stuttering. Images skipping and walls flickering

in Times Square: a tired reply to the Piazza
San Marco gleaming. How much more new world
there than this whipped-up tame light that

adds nothing to the secret of abstraction.

From C to D

Cleveland a clarioncall. Great American city
that charts its acres in my soul. On the east side
brick walls I dive straight in. I'm lost in contours
of the passing crowds.
                        Room on the sidewalks
broad streets. In the sky an unending blue.
That tall man in a coat could be Thomas Moran.
I'm going to start approaching men but I don't
know what I need.

At the house a lightning bolt with dozens of knees
tears open my eyes. Black fire escape. Black down
black up clambering line of flight like a migraine curse.
I am longing
            for my bloomhound.

Organs on show in the city. But sadly I don't know
what I need. The weight of my goal is too much
for my back. Never see it head on. Mirages at every
turn. Going astray. The west keeps moving away.

Can it be called destination if the city loses itself
in me? A hat-tall man full-beard in the smile
of a glorious *citoyen* and I seize my
chance:
                    have you given your fireblood today?
No. Like a word from the rooftops. From an insight
into the private geographies of the city's rim. I fall
on my wrist.

Put your hands on your head I tell myself. Turn
the way leave. Cleve-land. Leaveland. Your ticket
expires in some unknown part of the city.

                    I missed my rescue

an imported guesthouse a grave yard. Places
shown to me for my delight: leave this step
to me the new stillness in my legs.
                    Racing in slo-mo.

Industry viewed from the bridge. A huge harbour.
Across the rooftops arteries silvering in the sun.
Brick walls with sharp shadows.

'You might not remember any of this.
                    I'm holding
your hand.' This way I won't you won't be lost.

Denver. December. That's where I must go.

Vita Poetica

It is long years since yesterday and how much I've
forgotten about those slow sentences in which I

leaned over sideways and a motive gave me my
answer it is long years since yesterday who had

such delicate fingers for questions when we'd
diagnose into the night: where is infra-blue slept

where in my tongues the star-streaked kept? I've got
running sand in my shoes from all the seven-liners

and where's the flooded eye of someone else? Long
years since yesterday who held my arm and stood

by me: you are a head beauty a Russian one
with a melancholy soul if I may make so bold on the

Nevsky? Long years of that tiny private picking
and back to back sharing a single air a tree.

Follow Me I Said

Go on let all that lie the night
desire the pale mountain fire. Onions
in the bag the round browned paper.

Turning into a crystal-gazer with church
and soul. Godseeker through and through?
Kindling for the metaphysical comes

mostly from the day. That's where the
honey gathers. Where a nest is peopled.
Where dredger mouths gape and gasp

for air. That's where I'll teach you the beauty
of an 'and' in the first sittings of evening.
Ears not too shy to hear the secret. Something

left behind for you by the c.v. of the scree
even if it's black. Or streetsilver and a world
of reflections and threadstars and an egg.

Ars Poetica

Physics is Greek to me. Quantz's school of the flute.
A blackbird circling the word. Breathe in stop.

Carry on breathing. Find out what you do best
and leave it behind. Each time flesh thickens the

familiar gesture. My poetry loves the sex
of a man. We've got wine. I'm the woman.

Evensong. No need for second helpings or
old verse. Breathe in stop. Carry on breathing

and into the garden. The Roman hair of Frau von
Stein is pure physics. The sky empty. Swarms of stars

snuffed out before their light could tell us of the cold
and nights away from home. I want to understand

my counterpart in his formal suit. Breathe in
stop. Carry on breathing ahead of his time for

nothing. Quantz's theory for nothing or how come
all that's in a word keeps changing back and forth?

Notes on the Poems

p. 32. 'St Petersburg Poem: The Truth': Anna Akhmatova is buried in the Komarovo graveyard near St Petersburg. 'Most imaginary city' is Dostoevsky's description of St Petersburg.

p. 34. 'Lost Gardens of Heligan': Heligan House in Cornwall was used during the First World War as a home for soldiers recuperating from psychological trauma. The splendid gardens ran wild in the following decades and were reconstructed in the 1990s.

p. 36. 'If Bohemia Lies by the Sea': This refers to the poem 'Böhmen liegt am Meer' ('Bohemia lies by the Sea') by Austrian poet Ingeborg Bachmann.

p. 49. 'Plaits': The 8 May, now known as VE day, marks the formal acceptance by the Allies of World War II of Nazi Germany's unconditional surrender of its armed forces. The River Enns is a southern tributary of the Danube, which marked the boundary in Waidhofen, after the War, between the American and Soviet zones.

p. 57. 'Random Man': *Ein Bruderzwist in Hapsburg* is a famous play by Austrian dramatist Franz Grillparzer.

p. 64. 'Renaissance Song': For the 85th birthday of the Austrian poet Friederike Mayröcker on 20 December 2009. John Dowland (1563–1626), Elizabethan Lute player and composer, called himself ironically 'Semper Dowland, Semper Dolens' which suggests the pronunciation [ou]; on the basis of an unproven theory that he came from Ireland, the pronunciation [au] is also used.

p. 71. 'New York City Marathon': Paula Radcliffe, UK long-distance runner, who after a long time out of action on account of injuries and the birth of her daughter, won the New York City Marathon on 4 November 2007.

p. 78. 'About the Light (New York)': For his painting 'Snow Storm – Steam-Boat off a Harbour's Mouth' (1842) Joseph William Mallord Turner (1775–1851) is supposed to have had himself bound to the mast of the Ariel during a storm. 'Rain, Steam and Speed – The Great Western Railway' is the title of Turner's painting of 1844.

p. 79. 'From C to D': Thomas Moran (1837–1926), an American landscape painter, one of the Hudson River School.

p. 83. 'Ars Poetica': Johann Joachim Quantz (1697–1773), flautist, flute-maker, composer and flute teacher to Fredrick the Great. Author of the influential 1752 essay *On Playing the Flute*, a treatise on traverso flute-playing. Frau Charlotte von Stein was lady in waiting at the court of Weimar and a close friend of both Goethe and Schiller.

My First Plaits

Afterword by Evelyn Schlag

As a little girl I didn't know 'Europe'. There was my own country, Austria; beyond that the efficient Germany, which had once belonged to us, Russia, where the prisoners of war had worked and the bears lived and the moon stood over Siberia, and Italy, which was a happy country in the sun and at the sea. I had a pleasant fear of Africa and above all I had a sense of foreboding when I thought of America. In that eternal fifth year of my childhood I lived under the care of my beloved grandparents, in the same house, but one floor below ours because they had gone to America for a year. There my father wanted to study the art of anaesthetic. It was a big leap forwards such as wasn't possible at home. Americans moved about more freely. He hadn't left my mother any choice so she followed him and wrote sad letters home. In New York she had to keep two spoilt doctor's children from running to the swimming pool and drowning. In the evening they would jump into their beds with their boots on. My father worked for a tiny wage at a hospital. On a late November day in 1957 he was allowed to attend the birth of the presidential daughter Caroline at Cornell Medical Center. He was standing in the third row. I didn't quite understand why a stranger's daughter was more important to him than his own daughter. My grandfather was teaching me the art of writing so I could exchange letters with my mother – and the art of waiting.

I had refused to enter the building where the kindergarten was. In the entrance I had instinctively felt that so many unknown children in one place couldn't do me any good. I didn't have to be led into the playrooms to know my place was in the house of my grandparents, in my grandfather's leather shop, where I sat at a desk behind a wall of pock-marked pigskin suitcases. They stood upright in a row, like a giant's book shelf. I was invisible to anybody except my grandfather, but I could, while writing important invoices, overhear the customers tell my grandfather this and that. The high society of the town bought leather handbags and Japanese trays with brushes of black ink on them for flowers, a fashion which my grandfather had taken up on the advice of a friend in Vienna who knew about such things. The farmers from the surrounding hills came twice a week, on Tuesdays and Fridays, to get leather and shoe polish (one brand had a frog with a crown on its lid), and the upper parts of their working boots and mountaineers' shoes, which my mother was able to sew, and drive belts for their agricultural machinery and wooden nails – that eternal miracle, how could they keep things together? My grandfather explained to me that the old German script, Fraktura, had been broken into pieces by a horrible monster and had fortunately been mended, but their spiky shape told of the disaster.

When my parents and I, on our first trip to Italy, passed through a little town in the Alps called Heiligenblut (Blood of the Saints) I immediately saw the terrifying wooden drops of blood on the miserable statues in our town's four churches. They must have committed extraordinary crimes to have been subjected to such torture. My most intense hope was that Jesus might not abuse me for his suffering which didn't concern me, in which I didn't have a hand. Nor had I begged for redemption. We never had a family Bible.

My early distrust of clerical personnel was confirmed when the prelate in my first year at school asked me what profession I would like to have one day – an amazing question at that time. I replied 'a dressmaker'. I wanted to become a dressmaker like the kind lady in her cosy, *salon*-like shop, where it always seemed to be autumn, which, however, could have had to do with her age. A dressmaker? I can still hear how the prelate's voice rose and fell on the last syllable. What might he have expected – a secretary, a primary school teacher?

The first thing I did when we arrived at the destination of our Italian vacation was to fall in love with our waiter. I mean to say no less than that was the first love of my life, the first man who made me aware of something unknown to me: the desire to talk to him and to be looked at in a way that showed his search for something in me which would prove that I was different from the rest of the little ladies.

In his black trousers and white waiter's jacket he danced from table to table, with an elegant spring in his step, an apparition from an alien world and yet undoubtedly a man, remotely related to other men. From my parents' movie programmes I knew so-called handsome men. These programmes didn't show them in real-life colours but in a monochrome bluish-green, or a dark violet or dark blue. There were no brown movie programmes. Those monochrome leaflets correlated with the chiffon scarves of my grandmother. Since she didn't know which colour a new movie programme would be she could never tune her scarves to them. Colours carried the world on their hands. My waiter with the sunburnt face didn't have to dress up in the first place.

Even before we went down to the breakfast room I pondered whether I should go in front of my parents or beside my mother, behind my mother or by myself. It could help him to prepare to greet me unwatched by my parents, raising his eye brows, a signal of recognition in his eyes, those black Italian eyes in the gorgeous face. When he finally approached our table to bow and ask about egg and jam his whole Italian nature enwrapped me as if we shared a dream. In this dream I and he had a common purpose, wanted something from each other, be it just the word 'jam'. He did everything in an Italian way. I felt the manner in which he poured the coffee into my parents' cups to be Italian. Most probably everything was new because at home I didn't visit coffee houses. We never ate anywhere but at home, my father had a sensitive stomach, couldn't bear tomatoes. Coffee, yes.

My gaze was fixed on the waiter's back when he collected plates from other tables or folded a spoilt table cloth. When on occasion he didn't see me because he was distracted my heart sank to the bottom of the sea. He only ever existed in his white jacket and black trousers.

I didn't think much about his age. Of course he was older than me, but he wasn't as old as my father, one could still marry him.

At the time I may have thought that all men younger than my father were available. For sure I lived in the same time as my Italian, one that was different from that of my father's with his history. Meeting somebody meant a simultaneity, therefore we had the same right to our emotions – is how I think about it today.

Saying goodbye was hard, but I didn't create a scene. Our hands touched for the first and last time, he promised to write to me – could it be that he had by magic stored my address in his white pocket? Luckily enough my father didn't overhear the small exchange, then it was off and back home. My heartache didn't last very long, I turned to collecting stamps, and the serious side of life began.

Sometimes I saw a motorcycle with a driver like a large black beetle bowed over the handlebars, in the sidecar a dog with his nose high up in the wind or a woman, headscarf tightly bound under her chin and large sunglasses. The lady sawn in half in the circus. When I put the end of my right plait in my mouth and then wrapped it round my finger, a so-called 'Schiller's curl' was formed. I knew that Schiller was the younger brother of Goethe and had blond curls. Goethe had white hair. Schiller was at least fifty years younger.

My parents' year in America has never vanished from my life. It took a seat on various chairs in my texts. Time and again it gets up and looks for a different seat or a sofa. It certainly has become a private myth and paved the way into English and also American literature as well, before I learned to speak English.

* * *

On 11 October 2001 I flew to Washington to where I was to be writer-in-residence at a little city college in Pennsylvania. I had been in the United States a couple of times before, but this was in the wake of nine-eleven. All that summer I had tortured myself over the issue of a visa, having received contradictory information. Would I need a special visa or only a visa-waiver like all other lecturers? (With my imperfect grasp of English spelling, I pictured a tall man kindly waving to me, visa in hand.) In my panic I filled in the strange card that asks you to set a cross against very intimate questions, such as whether you have committed a crime or planned a terrorist attack. I put a cross by 'business trip'. After all, I was getting paid for my stay and a lecture. Big mistake. After two hours of waiting, interrogation and further waiting, during which it was noted that my writer's (maiden) name – the one on my books – didn't correspond with my passport (married) name, I was released into real America. I was met by my friend who was waving a Stars 'n' Stripes towel and the officer told me one last time: 'You may have a car, you may have a house, but you must *not* take any physical money.' To which I replied: 'I want a dog.'

From my study on the upper floor of the college I could see a brick chimney with a nice white cap of whipped cream on it. There was a corner where I would sit for hours a day pondering the poems I was going to write. The other window looked down on the parking lot at the Bosler Free Library. On Sundays families would march to the library, each member carrying a book. I later got *The Ezra Pound Debate* there for a dollar because, as so often, an academic whose turn was over had had to get rid of baggage. I was there to work in gorgeous morning light. Alas, there never was an addition to my Elizabeth Bishop library in the adjacent second-hand-book store.

A year later I finally found my way to Elizabeth Bishop's family Bible. It was kept in the archive of Acadia University of Wolfville in Nova Scotia. I couldn't believe my eyes and my hands that touched the bulky brown book and opened it. *The New Devotional and Practical Pictorial Family Bible, containing the Old and New Testaments, Apocrypha, Concordance, and Psalms in Metre. Translated out of the Original Tongues, with all former Translations diligently Compared and Revised. Embellished with over 2,000 fine scripture illustrations.* That line clearly proved that I was in the right place, looking at the source of Bishop's long poem 'Over 2,000 Illustrations and a Complete Concordance'. Fortunately, the Bible reeked strongly of something that I couldn't make out.

Its solid cover had a central piece shaped like a sheep skin with round indentions where the head and legs of the animal had been cut off. My grandfather had stored staples of such hides in many colours. That very shape was the trade sign of leather dealers that hung outside the shops: metal boards with four different colours in the hide as if it were a map for four countries meeting along artificially drawn straight borders. This association came much later, as did the idea of an agnus dei.

There were etchings that spread over a whole page. Other pages that were made up of several scenes 'arranged in cattycornered rectangles'. They showed scenes from the Old and the New Testament and what 'unleavened bread' looked like; they explained idioms like 'a pillar of salt', old sun dials, Egyptian jewels, Daniel interpreting the 'Writing on the Wall' with a beam of light like a modern lecturer, maps of the Holy Land, views of towns, Jerusalem at the time of David seen from the south, and about the Garden of Eden it had to admit that its exact location as described in the account of the creation 'is not known with certainty at this day'. But the scientific research pointed to the highlands south of the Caucasus as the primeval seat of the human race.

In a letter to my publisher I marvelled over this pragmatic approach to faith. 'Everything being explained, no mystery left, no mystery about words either it seems.' At the time I considered it almost stifling for the imagination of a child; it might diminish the power of words. Was there a mysterious connection between Kuala Lumpur and koala? Or the endlessly fascinating word 'mezzanine' (from Italian *mezzo*) used in Austria for the slightly lower-ceilinged intermediate floor between ground floor and first floor in houses in Vienna. These were introduced in large numbers in the second half of the nineteenth century with the purpose of keeping the official number of floors down to minimize taxes. A mezzanine featured in the Viennese address of that Japanese tea-tray friend of my grandfather.

'One thing I noticed in the Archive. When I went through the Bible, there is a family page, or rather four of them, in the latter half, you know the kind of fold-out page that says Marriages, Births, Deaths, and the first one has a marriage certificate of the first couple that owns the Bible. The characters (letters) saying this are in white and blue and look like something swimming and half drowning in water, and then it suddenly dawned on me: "and painfully, finally that ignite in watery prismatic white-and-blue"'.

This is from the first part of Bishop's long poem 'Over 2,000 Illustrations and a Complete Concordance', which we know refers to her family Bible.

The eye drops, weighted, through the lines
the burin made, the lines that move apart
like ripples above sand,
dispersing storms, God's spreading fingerprint,
and painfully, finally, that ignite
in watery prismatic white-and-blue.

I continued: 'Have a look at "Over 2,000" please and tell me if it makes sense to read the last lines of the first stanza as referring to those pages. I could never quite make sense of them. This was really the single most exciting thing about the Bishopry, as exciting as seeing Great Village.' To which my publisher replied: 'Was it actually illustrated, and were the edges gilded? It makes perfect sense, and the more perfect if it was not any old concordance but the Family Bible, where she is seeing purpose and continuity and has nothing, alas, to add.'

'The concordance is just before the back, I had overlooked it for two days and was wondering what it actually was', I wrote back. 'There are 44 pages with 5 columns each. It lists the keywords alphabetically for passages in the Old and New Testaments. First word:

ABASE. Make low.

Job 40, 11. every one proud abase.

Isa.31,4. Lion will not abase himself.

Ezek. 21.26 – exalt him that is low and abase him that is high.

I noticed too that the edges are NOT gilded. 'The illustrations are plenty, but not in colour, in fact the only coloured thing is the family pages.'

And then there was that little red plastic box among Bishop's legacy, along with her will and the first editions. The size and shape reminded me of something I knew only too well from my childhood. The brown print on the little red box read ½ – 1 – 1½ – 2 cc. I opened it and there they were: Aunt (Nurse) Grace's syringes and two hypodermic needles made of stainless steel. My own boxes, back in the 1960s, were metal. The stainless steel needles and the syringes might just have been taken out of my mother's and my distillation machine in our kitchen, where these sets were cleaned twice a week. I had written a story about my traumatic experiences when, in 1964, I was found to be diabetic just like my mother a year before. I was twelve at the time. The red plastic box was the only object Aunt Grace took with her on her retirement in the 1960s.

* * *

I am very well aware that I have a penchant for 'tragic' writers, usually women. The danger of appropriating an aspect of another writer's biography or ways of seeing is apparent. But I can't deny a deep kinship with Katherine Mansfield, with whom I shared a biographical aspect (tuberculosis) and a fascination with Marina Tsvetaeva, whose complete dedication to her emotions was reflected in her sometimes eruptive style. Her letters show her vulnerability for – usually – men who couldn't reciprocate in their limited ability to love. '*A little* of me – and Rilke and Pasternak – I cannot imagine', she wrote to one of her lovers. The dramaturgy of her letter-passions is repeated again and again. She insists on loving according to her own measure. 'Do not wonder about my gigantic step towards you, it's the only one I have.' And each time the inevitable disappointment recurs.

As a child is growing up it keeps encountering new faces, new animals' shapes, clouds that are escaped animals, and it also makes them speak with distinct voices. That stuffed animals have conversations among themselves and with me and my mother has always been a fact. I wonder if the children I haven't had would have liked to talk to these personalities or whether they would have dismissed such baby talk (though it isn't baby talk) as silly. One of my teddy bears has a yellowish skin and was a chain smoker. The other one is missing a leg. He lost it in the war.

I am a patient observer, will stand motionless at the old glass door to the balcony of our 1915 home and watch the birds coming to their house. There is a nuthatch with its long bill, the heavy make-up of its black eye-stripe, the blue-grey upper parts of head and shoulders, its white throat and its beautiful orange-coloured breast and underside. All my nuthatches have been called Carlos Kleiber, like the conductor, the reason being its German name 'Kleiber'. This is related to the verb 'kleben', to fix something with one's spit, which is what nuthatches do to make the holes of their nests in trees smaller. He wouldn't listen to *Sitta europaea* of course. Come to think of it, the black stripe somehow suggests the outfit of a conductor.

There are set conversations, little dialogues with a certain woodpecker. I say: How's your head today? – Fine. No migraine. – Oh that makes me happy. – And you, he will ask. Any problems with missing nail files or the charger for your smart phone? – Surprisingly enough, there hasn't been an incident with either of the two so far, I will reply, on a lucky day.

Respectfulness has a number of merits. In the Dallas Museum of Art I once fell in love with a painting by Andrew Wyeth titled *That Gentleman*. It shows Wyeth's neighbour Tom Clark, a very tall, thin man, sitting on a wooden chair with only a few specks of blue paint having survived, his legs stretched out towards an oven from which the glow of a fire lights up the dark right-hand side of the painting. There is part of a board on the wall that shows two pairs of scissors neatly hung up by one handle. The legend said 'that gentleman' was the name the character gave to his tools because he had such high respect for them. (When they functioned,

I assumed.) Only recently I learned that he would also address a potato and even an annoying fly buzzing overhead as 'that gentleman'. Recent information in the Dallas MFA says that the artist wrote admiringly of his sitter: 'His voice is gentle, his wit keen, and his wisdom enormous. He is not a character, but a very dignified gentleman who might otherwise have gone unrecorded.'

There was no postcard or art print at the time. Back home I located the only book that included it and ordered it from Peter Tafuri, *Frost Pocket Farm, Books, Organic Produce and Cold Weather* in Pennsylvania. Mr Tafuri replied immediately: 'The book will be mailed. Since it's not too heavy, the shipping charge will only be $3. I'll pay any additional charge; Mozart is playing on the radio, and after giving him to the world, it's the least I can do for one of his fellow citizens!' What a gentleman. I wrote a poem for both.

* * *

To my mind a poet should by nature be an adventuress. One cannot reduce the specific lyric language of a writer down to a language of use. I firmly believe that you don't have to comprehend the poem the moment you are reading it. It is also interesting how those particles of a poet's experience fit together. The language of the poems can lead the reader to be interested in the contents.

Not that I would want to undervalue or diminish the communicative function of language. This is not my intention. It has to do with a process that made me concentrate more on the powers within language. Let the lines, words, sentences arrange themselves and watch the peculiar flow they bring to life. No hocus pocus, only the magic of poetic speech. A homage to form nevertheless. For the reader it can be a liberation to detect what is hidden in line after line. I love responses that tell of such moments and the astonishment and wonder they provide for an audience.

Words have bodily, visceral qualities, they experience space very sensitively. In my neologisms they often move closely up to each other, in other cases they vehemently protest against their neighbourhoods. Unexpected enjambment gives my lines the freedom to move on, breathe on into the next line and also across stanzas. Enjambment is one of the advantages of poetic language as compared to prose. I need to be absolutely free to decide what a line looks like. Stanza forms often develop between version 7 and 8 and are done away with in version 12 only to return in versions 17 to 18.

We all know that language and reality are two things. Language always creates something new, something other than reality. Knowing this gives me freedom or allows me to take liberties. You can *make* new things with language, you can softly push reality a little to the side, and still there are referential markers that will remain. It is about looseness, lightness. Lightfootedness. To some degree language is relieved of its referentiality, it grows wings when you leave part of the leadership in experience to language.

What fascinates me is what in German is called *leichtsinnig, Leichtsinn* – 'foolish' is only one aspect. It is something different from lightness as in 'The Unbearable Lightness of Being', it hints at frivolity.

Over the years and collections in my native German I have had different phases concerning form, like all writers. I wrote sonnets after I translated Douglas Dunn and still do so occasionally with great amusement. I do not believe in the value of a strict distinction between various registers. I mix neologisms with newly made old-fashioned words. I love to express disrespect hidden in wordplay. Idioms for me are there to be distrusted, played with, by which process their real meaning may all of a sudden become quite obvious. This is part of the heritage and tradition of an Austrian writer for whom scepticism of language has always been essential.

Sometimes a sentence will cross my way without my having worked at it. All of a sudden there is 'what will become of Anna's child' and gradually it finds its place. It is (again) a fairy-tale sentence but in the context of my poem it is deeply cynical. I do not need to know who Anna's child is. A poem like 'Thoughtsnow Drifting' describes a mood that is setting in when it starts snowing, a quiet murmuring that occurs parallel to the events of the outside world. 'My first plaits were the hair of fairy tales. I was not yet brunette and thought in blond'.

In my prose I have repeatedly written about encounters, unplanned and unexpected ones that change the lives of the persons concerned. Encounter and seduction. For a short time everything is possible, biographies are at one's disposal. Distances, words or whole sentences thrown out like bait that can reduce those distances in a moment and creat a closeness that may be taken seriously as an experiment. They told each other their signs of the zodiac. First shortcuts, first aberrations.

Sometimes I use English words in my German poems when I am in need of a rhyme. Words fall in love with each other. I like to address a beloved person: 'I love each and every finger on your hand'. – 'Now we know one another / by our underarms where our skin is not ashamed.' – Or the male town of St Petersburg. 'Always telling each other life stories – right? Asking: 'When will it be the Tuesday after winter?' And it is thrilling to lend my voice to a high-pressure front called Leo who is pleading to an Atlantic depression called Helène, 'I wanted you to see the town Tarifa'.

* * *

There has always been some pressure on artists to declare themselves – what about politics? I ask myself what that means for politics and imagination. In principle I do not think that the arts – any art – should feel obliged to demonstrate political engagement. In principle art and politics are two very different spheres, and it isn't the task of politics, or a social environment, or society itself, to put pressure on the Arts. Art is *per se* different from the social world, and one needn't evoke *l'art pour l'art* for this. No rules, no commands. I may talk about trees as long as I like. The free Western World or what may have remained of it by the time this book will be published allows us a privilege that not many countries enjoy. We can speak out for our political agenda without being tortured or killed. This can change almost overnight.

If a piece of political art doesn't include some general human aspect that is recognizable apart from its contents, it will soon be outdated; and in any case, as with certain poems, it needs notes. My suspicion is that due to the speed of our fractured and over-connected daily lives the memory span for people and events will gradually sink over the next decades. Teachers have been telling us this for years now. I used to think that my memory is a vast expanse of land with forests and caves and other hiding places and that sometime the need to get rid of names, for example, will naturally clean up a bit here, a bit there. Judging by the amount of data I have lost, and I cannot at any point even say how much that is, I should have a lot of free spaces now, ready to take in and let grow new names, fresh information, springtime arrivals. But what happens is quite the contrary.

Data are prone to become outdated, one might even say that this is their inevitable fate. What once was the source of enlightenment, a free mind eager to learn about what is outside its range without restrictions set by authoritarian rulers or clerical elites, is under a huge threat. Collecting information has become, not an obsession, but a daily routine to me. There's not a day when I do not add material to files on my computer, create new files, split up files. How will this affect my imagination, I wonder.

In this volume there is a poem called 'Poor Russia Song'. I started writing it soon after the Russian dissident Anna Politkowskaja had been shot and killed in October 2006 in Moscow. There had been an earlier attempt on her life when she wanted to report on the school massacre of Beslan. In her plane she had collapsed and was then diagnosed with multiple organ failure. This morning (and it could be any 'this' morning) I read about a colleague of Boris Nemzow (killed in Moscow late December 2015) named Vladimir Kara-Murza who was also poisoned twice, each time taking almost a year to recover. Multiple organ failure. Would I write a poem about Kara-Murza? Of course not, and not only because there is already my 'Poor Russia Song' of more than ten years ago. The anger is the same, but my imagination would not take it up now. I will follow up on Kara-Murza's life to come, whatever 'they' will grant him. On the second anniversary of Nemzow's murder in February 2017 the City of Moscow removed flowers, candles and photographs from the memorial site.

What if making somebody else's tragedy into art is a process that is inherently tainted or even corrupted by the transformation? Just as one has a responsibility towards a dead poet when one writes his or her biography, the interpretational liberties may harm the poems as stand-ins for biographical details. Can I pay tribute to Anna Politkovskaya's outstanding courage and humanity by writing four short lines, using a play on words? Even more disturbing, is it 'correct' to create a faux Russian name for the anonymous widow of an Islamist terrorist, Tchadorkovskaya, thus denying her an individual fate? I wanted this woman to contain both her faith and the territories of post-Soviet republics such as Chechnya.

The impulse for a new poem may come from a newspaper clipping, the reliable source for 'unheard-of incidents' that we also find in novellas with their sudden plot turns. Or from a video in an online paper, something that arouses my curiosity and captures my imagination. Such was the case with the outrageous incident of a fifteen-year-old girl in a Seattle Metro tunnel who was assaulted by another teenage girl while security personnel and other passengers were watching without trying to help the victim. The surveillance video made the news world-wide. In the contract for the security firm it says that their staff was not allowed to take action.

In 2006 I came across an article titled 'Twenty-four Israel Defense Forces soldiers were killed in heavy clashes with Hezbollah forces in South Lebanon'. The article listed all of them by name, giving them their *curricula vitae* and adding commentaries by their comrades and friends. The first name was that of Staff Sergeant Uri Grossman, twenty, of Mevasseret Zion. He was the son of David Grossman, the renowned novelist and peace activist. When I read through that four-page list what struck me was a recurring formula: He is survived by. Parents and six siblings, parents and his brother, and so on. The unspeakably sad litany of those left behind haunted me and soon after I began my poem 'Genealogy News'. I was trying out ways to incorporate these set pieces into short glimpses of 'normal' daily life. 'Smart exit / the little garden gate falls to behind the lost / son. When he's back he'll get round to mending it // and leaves behind his parents and two sisters.'

Once I start taking down a few words the aesthetic challenge takes over. I like to let language have its way. Words arrange themselves to their liking, seeking sounds, alliterations, longing for an inner rhyme. In this way, too, it is possible to write poems critical of society, reconciling innovation and – awful word – message. I may feel the urge to write a sonnet about what is happening to our teens and find the form supports the content. The power of global fashion labels that produce uniforms for millions of young not-yet individuals in criminal sweatshops; peer pressure; the administration of leisure time by uncontrolled and uncontrollable mega-complexes; the colonisation of consciousness by computer games; the transformation of parents into mere providers of the latest electronic gadgets.

What's wrong with the admirable Poetry Foundation's suggestions of 'Poems of Anxiety and Uncertainty. Confronting and Coping with Unchartered Terrains through Poetry'? Of course nothing is wrong with that. The editors assure us that poets are by nature on the lookout for new and unknown ways of coping with life, 'with uncertainties, ambiguities, and shades of grey'. Shades of grey? You can rest assured that the poems offered on that site are of high quality. As one example among others they suggest 'Little Exercise' by Elizabeth Bishop, which is meant to calm the imagination and at the same time conjures up a very vivid memory of Key West.

What gives me the creeps is when poetry is exclusively judged by its usefulness and usability. In the economically-coded art environments that are the rule nowadays, where politicians and art managers speak of 'creative locations', poetry is all too often swept aside.

Acknowledgements

Some of these poems previously appeared in *PN Review* and *Poetry Salzburg Review*.